MARGRET & H.A.

HOORAY FOR HALLOWEEN

Curious George

Illustrated in the style of H. A. Rey by Martha Weston
Previously published as *Curious George Goes to a Costume Party*

Houghton Mifflin Harcourt
Boston   New York

Previously published as *Curious George Goes to a Costume Party*

Curious George® is a registered trademark and the Curious George logo is a trademark of Houghton Mifflin Harcourt Publishing Company.

hmhbooks.com

The text was set in Adobe Garamond.
The illustrations are watercolor.

ISBN: 978-0-544-69956-4 hardcover
ISBN: 978-0-358-21177-8 paperback

SCP 10 9 8 7 6 5 4 3 2 1
4500794985

This is George.

He was a good little monkey and always very curious.

One day George and his friend, the man with the yellow hat, were on their way to a party at Mrs. Gray's house.

George could not wait. He liked parties, and he was
looking forward to seeing Mrs. Gray. But when the door
opened George did not see Mrs. Gray at all—he saw a witch!

"Don't be afraid, George," said the man with the yellow hat. "This witch is our friend."

The witch took off her mask. It was Mrs. Gray after all! "Oh dear," she said. "Did I forget to tell you this was a costume party?"

George had never been to a costume party before. Inside he saw more people that he knew. They were all wearing costumes. There was his friend Betsy dressed up like an astronaut. And was that Bill? Why, he looked just like a mummy!

George wanted to wear a costume, too.
"I have some dress-up clothes upstairs,"
said Mrs. Gray. "Would you like to use
them to make a costume, George?"

Mrs. Gray took George to a room with a big trunk filled with clothes.

"Borrow anything you like, George," she said. "I have just the thing for your friend downstairs."

George tried on lots of costumes.

The first was too big.

The next was too small.

Another was too silly.

And this one was too scary!

At last George found a costume that was just right. George was a rodeo cowboy! He wore a vest and pants with fringe. He even had a lasso and a hat!

If only he could see himself in the mirror.

George was curious. Could he see himself if he stood on the bed? No. He needed to jump higher.

George bounced on the bed—just a little—but still he couldn't see.

He bounced a little more, and a little more.

Soon George was having so much fun, he forgot all about looking
in the mirror. He bounced as high as he could until—

CRASH!—George bounced off the bed.
He smashed into the night table and
got tangled up in the tablecloth.
Suddenly everything went dark.

George heard the people
downstairs gasp, "What was
that?"
"Was that a ghost?"

A ghost?! George did not want to meet up with a ghost alone. He dashed out of the room and down the hall. He wanted to get back to his friend in a hurry and he knew the fastest way.

He hopped onto the
stair rail and sailed—
WHOOSH!—down
the stairs.

"It *is* a ghost!" someone screamed. Everyone turned. They looked scared, and they were looking at George. The ghost must be right behind him!

George flew off the rail and landed—PLOP!—in the arms of a
farmer. But this wasn't really a farmer. It was his friend, the man
with the yellow hat!

Soon everyone stopped looking scared and started to laugh.

"That's not a ghost. That's a cowboy!" laughed a policeman.
"That's not a cowboy. That's a monkey!" giggled a princess.
"That's not just any monkey," said Betsy. "It's Curious George!"
Everyone clapped and cheered. They liked George's Halloween trick.

"You gave us a good scare, George," said Mrs. Gray. "And I'm glad to see you found some interesting costumes. Now why don't I take your ghost outfit so you can join the party?"

After the guests bobbed for apples, lit jack o' lanterns, and played
some party games, prizes for the best costumes were handed out.

There was one prize for Betsy, and one
for Bill, and *two* for Curious George.

"You were the best ghost *and* the best cowboy, George," said Mrs. Gray.

Everyone had a good time at the party, especially George.
Too soon it was time to say goodbye.

"Good night, George."
Happy Halloween!